Desserts

MANDY WAGSTAFF

MEREHURST

LONDON

Contents

Managing Editor: Janet Illsley
Photographer: Alan Newnham
Designer: Sue Storey
Food Stylist: Mandy Wagstaff
Photographic Stylist: Maria Jacques
Typeset by Angel Graphics
Colour separation by Fotographics, UK - Hong Kong
Printed in Italy by New Interlitho S.p.A.

Published 1991 by Merehurst Ltd,
Ferry House, 51/57 Lacy Road, Putney, London SW15 1PR

© Merehurst Ltd

ISBN: 1 85391 143 7 (Cased)
ISBN: 1 85391 235 2 (Paperback)

NOTES
All spoon measures are level: 1 tablespoon = 15ml spoon;
1 teaspoon = 5ml spoon.

Introduction

Cooking is all about confidence. It is an art that takes practice to master, but once you have learnt the basic techniques you can let your imagination run wild. We all make mistakes from time to time, so don't be disheartened by the occasional disaster.

Particularly with desserts, it is vital to stick to the recommended ingredients, quantities and methods for basics such as cakes, doughs and batters. But by all means change the fillings, flavourings, sauces and finishing touches to suit your own taste. Likewise if there is a flavouring ingredient that is unavailable, don't hunt around for hours, find a suitable alternative instead.

When you are buying ingredients, select fresh ones in optimum condition: this does not necessarily mean the most expensive. Always choose ripe fruits that are in season as they will be far more delicious than those that have been forced in glasshouses, or picked unripe and flown in from afar. If you are lucky enough to grow your own fruits I am sure you will agree that there is nothing better than a warm, ripe native fruit straight from the tree.

It is always important to choose a dessert that will complement the rest of your meal. If you are having a heavy main course, end with a light sorbet or fruit dessert. If your main course is lighter, you could opt for one of the richer, more substantial puddings.

I believe most of us have a sweet tooth, even if we don't succumb to it. I hope you will relax and enjoy cooking my desserts, as I am sure your guests will enjoy eating them too!

Pears with Figs & Pomegranate

An ideal dessert for winter, featuring delicious fruits in a warming spicy syrup. A good robust red wine, such as St Emillion, is perfect for the syrup.

6 pears
3 figs
2 seedless oranges
1 pomegranate
WINE SYRUP:
2 bottles red wine
1 cinnamon stick
4 cloves
4 green cardamon pods

1 bay leaf
1 star anise
2 coriander seeds
2 white peppercorns
1cm (1/2 inch) cube fresh root
   (green) ginger, thinly sliced
90g (3oz/1/3 cup) soft brown
   sugar

1 To make the syrup, pour the wine into a large saucepan, bring to the boil and simmer, uncovered, until reduced by one third. Tie the spices in a square of muslin and add to the wine with the ginger and sugar. Continue to simmer until the liquid is reduced to half of its original volume.

2 Peel and halve the pears, then scoop out the cores, using a melon baller. Add them to the wine, cover with a disc of greaseproof paper and simmer for 15-20 minutes until the pears are tender. Quarter the figs, add to the hot syrup and leave to cool, so they absorb the flavours.

3 Peel and segment the oranges. Halve the pomegranate and scoop out the flesh.

4 Lift the pears and figs out of the syrup and place in a glass serving bowl. Add the orange segments and pomegranate flesh. Strain the syrup; taste and add a little more sugar if necessary. Pour the syrup over the fruit. *Serves 6.*

Peaches with Champagne Sauce

This impressive dish is easier to prepare than it looks. Sparkling wine can be used instead of Champagne.

4 firm ripe peaches
SYRUP:
½ bottle Champagne
1 vanilla pod
½ cinnamon stick
juice and pared zests of
* ½ orange and ½ lemon*
185g (6oz/¾ cup) caster sugar

SPUN SUGAR:
250g (8oz) lump sugar
100ml (3½ fl oz/½ cup) water
2 drops of lemon juice
CHAMPAGNE SAUCE:
3 egg yolks
90g (3oz/⅓ cup) caster sugar
5 tablespoons Champagne

1 Lower the peaches into a pan of boiling water for 20-30 seconds, then remove and peel off the skins.

2 Put the syrup ingredients in a pan and heat gently until the sugar is dissolved. Add the peaches and lay a disc of greaseproof paper on top. Cover and poach gently for 20 minutes or until the peaches are tender. Cool in the liquid.

3 To prepare the spun sugar, put the lump sugar and water in a heavy-based pan and heat gently until the sugar has dissolved. Add the lemon juice. Bring to the boil and simmer until the caramel is golden and registers 155C (305F) on a sugar thermometer. Allow to cool for 1 minute.

4 Support a clean, lightly oiled broom handle to jut out about 30cm (12 inches) from the work surface. Cover the floor below with newspaper. Hold two forks back to back, dip into the caramel and wave back and forth over the broom handle to form threads. Repeat to make plenty of spun sugar, warming the caramel to melt, as necessary.

5 When ready to serve, prepare the Champagne sauce. Place the egg yolks, caster sugar and Champagne in a large heatproof bowl over a pan of simmering water and whisk continually until the whisk leaves a ribbon when lifted. Remove the bowl from the heat and whisk until cool. Thin the sauce with a little of the poaching liquid.

6 Drain the peaches and place on serving plates. Surround with Champagne sauce and top with spun sugar. *Serves 4.*

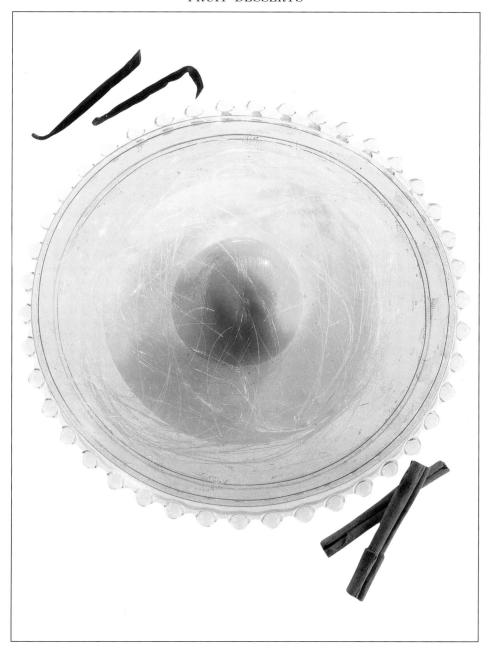

Fig Gratin

A simple yet sophisticated dessert. Accompany with a glass of chilled Champagne for the perfect end to a summer meal.

6 ripe figs
3 egg yolks
1 tablespoon honey
3 tablespoons white wine

315ml (10 fl oz/1¼ cups)
whipping cream
155ml (5 fl oz/⅔ cup) port
TO FINISH:
icing sugar for dusting

1 Preheat the grill to high and lightly butter 6 heatproof plates. Peel the figs and cut each one into 8 wedges. Arrange on individual plates.

2 Place the egg yolks, honey and white wine in a large heatproof bowl and whisk until evenly mixed. Place the bowl over a pan of boiling water and continue to whisk until the mixture is thick enough to leave a ribbon when the whisk is lifted. Remove the bowl from the heat and whisk until cool.

3 Whisk the cream lightly until it is almost thick enough to leave a ribbon, then fold into the egg mixture together with the port, being careful to avoid over-mixing.

4 Spoon this mixture over the figs as evenly as possible and place each plate under the grill for about 1 minute until golden brown.

5 Dust with a little icing sugar and serve immediately.
Serves 6.

NOTE: If the figs are under-ripe, it may be necessary to poach them in a little sugar syrup before assembling the gratin.

Summer Fruit Meringue Nests

To ensure the cream and chocolate sauce ripple to maximum effect they must be the same consistency; if necessary whip the cream slightly.

MERINGUE NESTS:
2 egg whites
pinch of salt
125g (4oz/½ cup) caster sugar
CHOCOLATE SAUCE:
155ml (5 fl oz/⅔ cup) milk
100g (3½ oz) dark chocolate

15g (½ oz) butter
TO FINISH:
155ml (5 fl oz/⅔ cup) whipping cream
250g (8oz) raspberries
250g (8oz) redcurrants

1 Preheat the oven to 120C (250F/Gas ½). Line 2 baking trays with non-stick paper and mark two 10cm (4 inch) circles on each.
2 In a large grease-free bowl, whisk the egg whites with the salt until stiff peaks form. Add half of the sugar a spoonful at a time, whisking well between each addition. Carefully fold in the remaining sugar, using a spatula, to give a very stiff and glossy meringue.
3 Transfer the meringue to a piping bag fitted with a 1cm (½ inch) fluted nozzle. Pipe over each marked circle, starting at the centre and working outwards in a spiral. Pipe 1 or 2 more layers around the edge.
4 Bake in the oven for 2 hours or until firm. Transfer to a wire rack and allow to cool.
5 To make the chocolate sauce, pour the milk into a small pan and bring to the boil. Remove from the heat, add the chocolate, let stand for 2 minutes, then stir until smooth. Add the butter and set aside to cool.
6 Pour a pool of cream on to each individual plate. Drizzle the chocolate sauce around the edge and work with a skewer to give a rippled effect. Stand the meringue nests on top and fill with raspberries and redcurrants. Serve immediately.
Serves 4.

Fruit Brochettes

This simple dessert can be flambéed, barbecued or served chilled. Change the fruits according to the season, to ensure they are ripe and full of flavour.

8 strawberries
16 lychees
16 cherries
1 papaya
2 figs
16 small bay or mint leaves

MARINADE:
grated rind and juice of 1 lime
2 tablespoons honey
1 teaspoon green peppercorns
TO SERVE:
4 tablespoons kirsch
250ml (8 fl oz/1 cup) crème
fraîche

1 Halve the strawberries but do not hull them. Stone the cherries; peel and stone the lychees. Peel the papaya and cut into even-sized chunks. Cut the figs into quarters. Place all the fruits in a shallow dish.

2 In a small bowl, mix together the lime rind and juice, honey and peppercorns. Pour over the fruits and leave to marinate for 2 hours.

3 Lift the fruits out of the marinade and thread alternately on to 8 skewers. Add a bay or mint leaf to each skewer.

4 Place the skewers under a preheated grill for 2-3 minutes, if desired, then arrange in a flameproof serving dish. Warm the kirsch in a small pan, pour over the brochettes and set alight. Serve at once. *Serves 4 or 8.*

NOTE: Before using wooden skewers it is best to soak them in water for several hours. This prevents them burning under the grill or on the barbecue.

Summer Fruit Salad

Serve this dessert to refresh the palate at the end of a meal. Select fruits with flavours and colours which complement one another. Ensure they are fully ripe so there is no need to add sugar.

FRUITS IN SEASON:
2 kiwi fruit
1 papaya
1 star fruit
2 nectarines
125g (4oz) raspberries
8 strawberries
2 passion fruit (optional)

MANGO SAUCE:
1 large ripe mango
1 tablespoon lemon juice
1 tablespoon honey
TO DECORATE:
mint sprigs

1 First make the mango sauce. Peel and roughly chop the mango, discarding the stone. Place in a blender or food processor with the lemon juice and honey and work to a smooth purée; set aside.

2 To prepare the fruits, peel and slice the kiwi fruit and papaya. Slice the star fruit and nectarines. Pick over the raspberries; halve the strawberries but do not hull. Halve the passion fruit, if using, and scoop out the flesh.

3 Spoon a pool of mango purée on to each dessert plate and arrange the fruits attractively on top. Decorate with mint sprigs to serve. *Serves 4.*

Rum Savarins with Fruit

90g (3oz/³/₄ cup) strong white
   flour
pinch of salt
3 tablespoons milk
7g (¹/₄ oz/1¹/₂ teaspoons) fresh
   yeast, or 1 teaspoon dried
1 teaspoon caster sugar
1 egg, lightly beaten
45g (1¹/₂ oz) butter

SYRUP:
90g (3oz/¹/₃ cup) caster sugar
155ml (5 fl oz/²/₃ cup) water
pared rind of 1 lemon
few drops of lemon juice
1 tablespoon framboise liqueur
TO SERVE:
250g (8oz) raspberries
mint leaves

1 Grease 4 individual 10cm (4 inch) ring moulds; set aside.

2 Sift the flour and salt into a large bowl and make a well in the centre. Heat the milk until lukewarm, then mix in the yeast and sugar. Add the egg to the milk, then pour into the well in the flour. Sprinkle a little of the flour over the liquid and leave to stand in a warm place for 15-20 minutes or until the yeast starts to bubble.

3 Melt the butter and cool slightly before adding to the liquid ingredients. Using a wooden spatula, mix all the ingredients together. Continue beating with the spoon or by hand until a slack, glossy dough is formed. Pour into the prepared moulds and allow to stand in a warm place for 1 hour or until doubled in size.

4 Preheat the oven to 200C (400F/Gas 6). Bake the savarins for 10-15 minutes or until an inserted skewer comes out clean. Turn out on to a wire rack and leave to cool.

5 To make the syrup, heat the sugar and water gently in a small pan to dissolve the sugar. Add the lemon rind and juice, bring to the boil and cook for 1 minute. Remove from the heat and add the liqueur.

6 Immerse the savarins in the syrup, one at a time, then return to the wire rack placed over a tray to collect any drips. Dab any remaining syrup over the savarins.

7 Place the savarins on individual plates and fill with raspberries. Decorate with mint leaves and serve with pouring cream. *Serves 4.*

Orange Soufflés

4 oranges
250ml (8fl oz/1 cup) milk
1 vanilla pod, split
3 egg yolks
60g (2oz/¼ cup) caster sugar
30g (1oz/¼ cup) plain flour
60ml (2fl oz/¼ cup) grand
   marnier

4 egg whites
TO SERVE:
2 pink grapefruit
3 passion fruit, halved
1-2 tablespoons honey
1 teaspoon arrowroot, blended
   with 2 teaspoons cold water

1 Preheat the oven to 200C (400F/Gas 6). Halve the oranges crosswise and carefully remove the segments, as though you were preparing a grapefruit. Remove the membrane from the orange shells and discard. Place the orange halves on a baking tray and divide the orange segments between them; set aside.

2 Put the milk and vanilla pod in a saucepan and bring to the boil. In a bowl, whisk together the egg yolks and all but 1 tablespoon of the sugar until thick and light. Lightly stir in the flour. Stir in a little of the hot milk, then add to the milk in the pan. Cook, stirring, for 1 minute until thickened. Stir in the grand marnier. Discard the vanilla pod.

3 Whisk the egg whites until stiff peaks form. Add the remaining 1 tablespoon of sugar and whisk for 1 minute. Lightly fold into the warm crême patissière.

4 Spoon the soufflé mixture into the orange shells. Bake for 7-10 minutes until well risen and golden.

5 Meanwhile, squeeze the juice from 1 grapefruit and place in a small pan with the passion fruit pulp and honey. Warm the sauce and skim the surface. Add the blended arrowroot and cook, stirring, until slightly thickened. Sieve to remove the passion fruit seeds if preferred. Peel and segment the other grapefruit.

6 Serve the soufflés immediately, surrounded by the sauce, and decorated with grapefruit segments. *Serves 4-8.*

Blackcurrant Parfait

Serve this refreshing mousse in tall glasses to show the layers. Use fresh or frozen blackcurrants.

500g (1lb) blackcurrants
315ml (10fl oz/1¼ cups) crème de cassis
15g (½oz/5 teaspoons) powdered gelatine
220g (7oz/⅞ cup) caster sugar

185ml (6fl oz/¾ cup) water
2 egg whites
315ml (10fl oz/1¼ cups) whipping cream
TO DECORATE:
blackcurrants and leaves

1 If using fresh blackcurrants, wash them and remove the stalks. Place a tablespoonful of blackcurrants in each of 6 glasses. Add a tablespoonful of the crème de cassis to each serving and set aside.

2 Put 2 tablespoons crème de cassis in a small heatproof bowl, sprinkle on the gelatine and leave until spongy.

3 Put 155g (5oz/⅔ cup) of the sugar in a small pan with the water and heat gently until the sugar has dissolved. Bring to the boil and cook for 1 minute.

4 Put the rest of the blackcurrants in a blender or food processor with half of the sugar syrup and the remaining crème de cassis and work to a purée. Pass through a fine nylon sieve, then pour two thirds into a bowl. Put the other third into another bowl, with the remaining sugar syrup.

5 Warm the gelatine over a pan of hot water until it has dissolved, then add half to each bowl of purée, stirring well.

6 Chill the two-thirds portion of purée until beginning to set. Meanwhile, whisk the egg whites until stiff peaks form, then gradually whisk in the remaining sugar until thick and glossy. Whip the cream until soft peaks form. Stir a little of the cream and meringue into the chilled purée to lighten it, then fold in the remainder. Spoon the mousse into the glasses, smooth the tops and chill until set.

7 Spoon the blackcurrant jelly over each mousse to cover. Allow to set, then decorate with blackcurrants and leaves. *Serves 6.*

Orange & Mint Jelly

*15g (¹/₂oz/5 teaspoons) powdered
  gelatine*
*500g (16fl oz/2 cups) fresh
  orange juice*

1 tablespoon grand marnier
about 40 mint leaves
10 oranges
mint sprigs to decorate

1 Soak the gelatine in 2 tablespoons orange juice until spongy. Bring the remaining orange juice to the boil in a pan and skim the surface. Add the gelatine and stir until dissolved. Add the grand marnier. Allow to cool.

2 Pour a 5mm (¼ inch) layer of jelly into a 940ml (1½ pint/ 3¾ cup) terrine. Chill until set. Wash and dry the mint leaves. Peel and segment the oranges, discarding all pith.

3 When the jelly has set, cover with a layer of mint leaves, then 2 layers of orange segments. Pour over enough jelly to cover and refrigerate until set. Add another layer of mint leaves followed by a further 2 layers of orange segments; set aside any remaining segments for decoration. Pour the remaining jelly over the top. Chill until firm.

4 To unmould, run a small knife around the sides of the jelly, dip terrine into hot water for a few seconds, then invert on to a plate. Cut into slices, using a sharp knife. Serve, decorated with orange segments and mint. *Serves 6-8.*

Tangy Lemon Mousse

*375ml (12fl oz/1½ cups)
  condensed milk*
*315ml (10fl oz/1¼ cups)
  whipping cream*

*grated rind and juice of
  4 large lemons*
lemon slices to decorate

1 Put the condensed milk and cream into a large bowl and whisk with an electric beater until thick enough to leave a ribbon. With the motor still running, slowly add the lemon rind and juice; the mixture will suddenly thicken. Immediately transfer to serving dishes. Chill overnight. *Serves 6-8.*

Chestnut Bavarios

This light bavarious makes the perfect alternative Christmas dessert. It can be made a day in advance, then turned out and decorated the following day.

7g (¹/₄oz/2¹/₂ teaspoons)
  powdered gelatine
250ml (8fl oz/1 cup) milk
250g (8oz) can unsweetened
  chestnut purée
3 egg yolks
90g (3oz/¹/₃ cup) caster sugar

250ml (8fl oz/1 cup) whipping
  cream
TO DECORATE:
whipping cream
3 marrons glacés, halved
icing sugar for dusting

1 Chill a 940ml (1½ pint/3¾ cup) charlotte tin. Soak the gelatine in 1 tablespoon water until spongy. Place the milk and half of the chestnut purée in a pan and bring to the boil. Whisk together the egg yolks and 60g (2oz/¼ cup) of the sugar until thick and light. Stir in a little of the hot milk, then add to the remaining milk in the pan and cook, stirring, until the custard thickens enough to coat the back of the spoon. Do not allow to boil.

2 Add the soaked gelatine to the hot custard; it should dissolve immediately. Chill until on the point of setting.

3 Whip the cream until soft peaks form and set aside. Place the remaining chestnut purée in a small bowl and break up with a fork. Add the remaining sugar and beat until smooth. Fold in 2 tablespoons of the chilled custard and 1 tablespoon of the cream. Set aside.

4 Fold the remaining cream into the chilled custard and pour half of this bavarois mixture into the charlotte tin. Refrigerate until set. Spoon the chestnut purée on to the set bavarios and spread evenly with the back of the spoon. Top with the remaining bavarois mixture and chill until set.

5 To unmould the bavarois, run the point of a knife around the top edge. Dip the mould into hot water for a few seconds, then invert on to a chilled plate. Decorate with whirls of cream and marrons glacés. Dust with icing sugar. *Serves 6.*

Praline Charlotte

PRALINE:
90g (3oz/⅓ cup) caster sugar
3 tablespoons water
90g (3oz/½ cup) blanched
  almonds, toasted
CUSTARD:
7g (¼oz/2½ teaspoons)
  powdered gelatine
250ml (8fl oz/1 cup) milk
1 vanilla pod, split

3 egg yolks
2 teaspoons caster sugar
250ml (8fl oz/1 cup) whipping
  cream
TO FINISH:
1 packet of sponge fingers
60g (2oz/¼ cup) caster sugar
60ml (2fl oz/¼ cup) water
2 tablespoons brandy
whipped cream

1 To make the praline, place the sugar and water in a small pan and heat gently until the sugar has dissolved. Bring to the boil and cook to a golden caramel, then quickly add the almonds. Pour the praline on to an oiled baking sheet. Leave to cool, then grind to a coarse, crunchy texture.

2 Soak the gelatine in 2 teaspoons water. Place the milk in a small pan with the vanilla pod and bring to the boil. Whisk the egg yolks with the sugar until thick and light. Stir in a little of the hot milk, then add to the remaining milk in the pan and cook until thickened enough to lightly coat the back of the spoon; do not boil. Discard the vanilla pod. Add the soaked gelatine and stir; it should dissolve immediately. Chill until on the point of setting, then fold in all but 1 tablespoon of the praline. Whip the cream until it forms soft peaks, then fold in to the custard.

3 Lay the biscuits sugary side down on the work surface. Place the sugar, water and brandy in a small pan and bring slowly to the boil. Moisten each biscuit with a little syrup. Use to line the sides of a 625ml (1 pint/2½ cup) soufflé dish, spooning in a little mousse to help them stand. Pour in the praline mousse and chill until set.

4 When set, trim the biscuits to the level of the mousse. Dip the soufflé dish into hot water for a few seconds, invert on to a chilled plate and shake to turn out. Decorate with piped cream and the remaining praline. *Serves 6.*

Soufflé Monte Cristo

125g (4oz) coffee beans
500ml (16fl oz/2 cups) milk
15g (¹/₂oz/5 teaspoons) powdered
  gelatine
6 tablespoons tia maria
6 egg yolks
75g (2¹/₂oz/5 tablespoons) caster
  sugar

375ml (12fl oz/1¹/₂ cups) double
  (thick) cream
2 egg whites
250g (8oz) ripe apricots
125g (4oz) ratafias
TO DECORATE:
whipped cream
apricot slices

1 Secure paper collars around 6 ramekins (see page 76). Coarsely grind the coffee beans and place in a heavy-based pan with the milk. Bring to the boil, remove from the heat and leave to infuse for 30 minutes. Soak the gelatine in 2 tablespoons tia maria until spongy.

2 Strain the milk through a nylon sieve lined with muslin. Return to the pan and bring back to the boil. Whisk the egg yolks and 60g (2oz/¹/₄ cup) of the sugar together until thick and light. Stir in a little of the boiling milk, then add to the milk in the pan and cook, stirring, until thick enough to coat the back of the spoon; do not boil.

3 Add the soaked gelatine to the hot custard and stir until dissolved. Cool until beginning to set.

4 Dip the apricots in boiling water for a few seconds to loosen the skins, then peel them. Halve and cut into slices. Soak the apricots and ratafias in the remaining tia maria.

5 Whip the cream until soft peaks form, then fold into the cold custard. Stiffly whisk the egg whites, add the remaining 1 tablespoon sugar and fold into the custard. Carefully spoon half of this mixture into the prepared ramekins, filling them slightly more than half full. Chill in the refrigerator until set.

6 Divide the apricot mixture between the ramekins and fill with the remaining soufflé mixture. Chill until set.

7 Carefully remove the paper collars and smooth the sides of the soufflés with a hot knife. Decorate the soufflés with piped cream and apricot slices. *Serves 8.*

Passion Fruit Tartlets

Passion fruit curd makes a pleasant change from lemon curd and it is just as simple to prepare.

125g (4oz/1 cup) plain flour
pinch of salt
60g (2oz) butter, in pieces
45g (1½oz/scant ¼ cup) caster
* sugar*
1 egg yolk
2 teaspoons water
1 drop of almond essence

PASSION FRUIT CURD:
4 passion fruit
125g (4oz/½ cup) caster sugar
125g (4oz) butter
3 eggs, beaten
1-2 teaspoons lemon juice
TO DECORATE:
1 passion fruit

1 To make the pastry, sift the flour and salt into a large bowl. Rub in the butter using the fingertips until the mixture resembles fine breadcrumbs. Stir in the sugar. Mix together the egg yolk, water and almond essence and add to the flour. Stir with a round-bladed knife until the dough clings together. Turn on to a lightly floured surface and knead gently until smooth. Wrap in plastic wrap and chill for 30 minutes.

2 Preheat the oven to 180C (350F/Gas 4). Roll out the pastry thinly and use to line four 10cm (4 inch) tartlet tins. Prick the bases with a fork. Line with greaseproof paper and dried beans. Bake blind for 10 minutes, then remove the baking beans and bake for a further 5 minutes until the pastry is dry. Allow to cool, then remove from the tins.

3 To make the fruit curd, halve the passion fruit and scoop the pulp into a heatproof bowl. Add the sugar and butter. Stand the bowl over a pan of simmering water and stir until the sugar has dissolved. Add the beaten eggs and cook, stirring for 7-8 minutes until the mixture thickens. Sieve and allow to cool slightly. Add lemon juice to taste. Divide the passion fruit curd between the tartlet cases. Leave to set.

4 To serve, halve the remaining passion fruit and spoon a little pulp on to each tartlet. *Serves 4.*

Summer Fruit Tartlets

500g (1lb) summer fruits, e.g.
* strawberries, blackberries,*
* blueberries; black, red and*
* white currants; figs, cape*
* gooseberries*
SWEET PASTRY:
125g (4oz/1 cup) plain flour
15g (¹/₂oz/2 tablespoons) ground
* almonds*
pinch of salt
60g (2oz) butter
60g (2oz/¹/₃ cup) icing sugar
1 egg yolk
1 drop of almond essence

CRÈME PATISSIÈRE:
250ml (8fl oz/1 cup) milk
1 vanilla pod, split
3 egg yolks
45g (1¹/₂oz/scant ¹/₄ cup) caster
* sugar*
45g (1¹/₂oz/¹/₄ cup) plain flour
knob of butter
TO GLAZE:
3 tablespoons apricot jam,
* sieved*
1 tablespoon water

1 Preheat oven to 180C (350F/Gas 4). Make pastry and use to line four 10cm (4 inch) tartlet tins as for passion fruit tartlets (page 30), adding the ground almonds with the flour, using icing sugar instead of caster sugar, and omitting the water. Bake blind for 10 minutes, then remove beans and paper and cook for 5 minutes. Cool, then remove from tins.

2 To make the crème patissière, place the milk in a saucepan with the vanilla pod and bring to the boil. In a bowl, whisk the egg yolks and sugar together until pale and thick, then stir in the flour. Pour a little of the hot milk on to the whisked mixture, then add to the milk in the pan. Bring to the boil and cook, stirring, for 2-3 minutes until thickened. Transfer the crème patissière to a plate to cool, dabbing the top with butter to prevent a skin from forming. Discard the vanilla pod.

3 Prepare the fruits: pick over the berries and currants; halve the larger strawberries; cut the figs into wedges; open up the cape gooseberries.

4 Divide the crème patissière between the 4 tartlet cases and arrange the fruits on top. Warm the apricot jam with the water and brush over the fruits to glaze. *Serves 4.*

Puff Pastry Hearts

250g (8oz) packet puff pastry
500g (1lb) rhubarb, washed and
   trimmed
grated rind and juice of
   1 orange
125g (4oz/½ cup) caster sugar

ALMOND CUSTARD:
250ml (8fl oz/1 cup) milk
3 eggs yolks
45g (1½oz/8 teaspoons) caster
   sugar
2 drops of almond essence
1 tablespoon amaretti liqueur

1 Roll out the pastry thinly on a lightly floured surface to a 5mm (¼ inch) thickness. Cut out 6 heart shapes, using a pastry cutter or by cutting round a homemade cardboard template. Place the pastry hearts on a baking sheet and chill for at least 30 minutes.

2 Preheat the oven to 230C (450F/Gas 8). Brush the top of each pastry heart with beaten egg and, using a sharp knife, mark on a criss-cross pattern. Bake for 7-10 minutes until crisp, golden and well risen.

3 Meanwhile, cut the rhubarb into 2.5cm (1 inch) batons. Place in a saucepan with the orange rind and juice and the sugar. Cook very gently for 4-6 minutes until the rhubarb is just tender, but holding its shape.

4 Meanwhile, make the custard: bring the milk to the boil in a small pan. Whisk the egg yolks with the sugar and almond essence until pale and thick. Pour on a little of the boiling milk, stir to mix, then add to the remaining milk in the pan. Cook, stirring, over a moderate heat until the custard thickens just enough to coat the back of the spoon; do not boil. Remove from the heat and add the liqueur and a little of the liquid from the rhubarb.

5 Halve the puff pastry hearts horizontally and scoop out any uncooked pastry. Place the bottom halves on warmed individual serving plates and spoon over the rhubarb using a slotted spoon. Position the pastry tops on the rhubarb and surround with the custard. Serve hot. *Serves 6.*

Wild Strawberry Shortcakes

Miniature wild strawberries – *fraise de bois* – are simply delicious. They may be expensive, but a few go a long way in this dessert and the taste sensation is well worth the cost.

ALMOND PASTRY:
250g (8oz/2 cups) plain flour
pinch of salt
30g (1oz/¼ cup) ground
  almonds
140g (4½oz) butter
100g (3½oz/⅔ cup) icing sugar
2 egg yolks
2 drops of almond essence

STRAWBERRY COULIS:
375g (12oz) strawberries
1-2 tablespoons icing sugar
juice of ½ lemon
  (approximately)
TO FINISH:
375g (12oz) wild strawberries
200ml (6fl oz/¾ cup) double
  (thick) cream
1 tablespoon icing sugar

1 Prepare the almond pastry as for passion fruit tartlets (page 30), adding the ground almonds with the flour, using icing sugar instead of caster sugar and omitting the water. Wrap in plastic wrap and chill for 30 minutes.

2 Preheat the oven to 190C (375F/Gas 5). Roll out the pastry thinly on a lightly floured surface. Using a 10cm (4 inch) fluted pastry cutter, cut out 12 rounds. Place on baking sheets and bake for 7-8 minutes until pale golden. Using a palette knife, transfer the pastry rounds to a wire rack to cool.

3 For the coulis, pureé the hulled strawberries in a blender or food processor. Add icing sugar and lemon juice to taste.

4 Reserve 4 wild strawberries with leaves for decoration; hull the remainder and set aside. Whip the cream with the icing sugar until soft peaks form.

5 To assemble the shortcakes: pipe cream on to 4 biscuits, top each with another biscuit and cover with a layer of wild strawberries and a spoonful of coulis. Dust remaining biscuits with icing sugar and place one on each shortcake.

6 Pour the remaining coulis on to individual serving plates and place a shortcake in the centre of each. Decorate with the reserved strawberries and leaves. *Serves 4.*

Hazelnut Cornucopias

Muscatels are large succulent raisins; they are often sold by the bunch. If unavailable use ordinary raisins instead.

CORNETS:
2 egg whites
90g (3oz/¹/₃ cup) caster sugar
60g (2oz/¹/₂ cup) plain flour,
sifted
60g (2oz) butter, melted
30g (1oz/¹/₄ cup) hazelnuts,
finely chopped
FILLING:
750g (1¹/₂lb) cooking apples
juice of 1 lemon

30g (1 oz) butter
1 tablespoon moist brown sugar
125g (4oz/³/₄ cup) muscatels,
soaked in diluted Calvados
dash of Calvados
CINNAMON CUSTARD:
250ml (8fl oz/1 cup) milk
4 cinnamon sticks
3 egg yolks
30g (1oz/2 tbsp) caster sugar
ground cinnamon for dusting

1 Preheat the oven to 190C (375F/Gas 5). Line 2 baking sheets with non-stick paper. Beat the egg whites with a fork until frothy. Stir in the sugar. Fold in the flour with the melted butter and chopped hazelnuts.

2 Spoon the mixture into 8 mounds on the baking trays, spacing well apart. Spread each one to a 10cm (4 inch) circle. Bake, one tray at a time, for 5-8 minutes until pale golden. Cool for a few seconds before lifting off with a palette knife and shaping each one round a cornet mould.

3 Peel, core and slice the apples; toss in lemon juice. Melt the butter in a large sauté pan until sizzling. Add the apples, sugar, muscatels and 2 teaspoons of the lemon juice. Cook over a moderate heat until the apples are softened but retain their shape. Add the Calvados and flambé.

4 To make custard, put the milk and cinnamon sticks in a pan and bring to the boil. Whisk egg yolks and sugar together until pale and thick. Stir in a little boiling milk, then add to the pan. Cook, stirring, until thickened. Discard the cinnamon.

5 To assemble, spoon the apple filling into the cornets. Pour a little custard on to each dessert plate, arrange 2 cornucopias on top and sprinkle with cinnamon. *Serves 4.*

Baked American Cheesecake

Personally, I prefer baked cheesecakes to the uncooked variety set with gelatine. For maximum flavour, allow this one to mellow over-night in the refrigerator before serving.

BASE:
125g (4oz) ginger biscuits
60g (2oz) butter
FILLING:
250g (8oz/1 cup) curd cheese
250g (8oz/1 cup) cream cheese
3 eggs
185g (6oz/³/4 cup) caster sugar
grated rind of 1 lemon
30g (1oz/¹/4 cup) plain flour
155ml (5fl oz/²/3 cup) soured cream

100ml (3¹/2fl oz/scant ¹/2 cup) whipping cream
2 tablespoons seedless raisins, soaked in 2 tablespoons brandy
TOPPING:
2 lemons
2 tablespoons honey
2 tablespoons water
2.5cm (1 inch) piece fresh root (green) ginger, sliced

1 Preheat the oven to 180C (350F/Gas 4). Lightly grease a 20cm (8 inch) springform tin. Place the biscuits in a plastic bag and crush them with a rolling pin. Melt the butter in a small pan and stir in the crumbs. Press the crumbs on to the base of the prepared tin, spreading them evenly with the back of a spoon. Set aside.

2 In a large bowl, mix together the curd cheese, cream cheese and eggs. Beat in the sugar and lemon rind. Fold in the flour, both creams and the raisins, with 1 tablespoon of the brandy. Spread over the base and bake for 45 minutes. Leave to cool in the switched-off oven for 30 minutes.

3 Score the lemons from top to bottom with a canelle knife, then slice thinly. Place in a pan with the honey, water and ginger. Cover with a disc of greaseproof paper and cook very gently for 20 minutes, until tender.

4 Drain the lemon slices, reserving the cooking liquid. Arrange the lemon slices around the top edge of the cheese-cake. Reduce the reserved liquid until syrupy, strain and lightly brush over the lemon slices and top of the cheesecake. Refrigerate overnight. Remove from the tin to serve. *Serves 8.*

Apple & Blackberry Filo Pie

Filo is one of the easiest pastries to use as it doesn't require rolling out. Here it makes a welcome change from shortcrust pastry to encase a pie filling. My recipe suggests making a large pie, but you could try making individual ones if you prefer.

1kg (2lb) cooking apples
juice of 1 lemon
185g (6oz) butter
60g (2oz/¹/₃ cup) moist brown
  sugar

10 sheets filo pastry, measuring
  36 × 18cm (14 × 7 inches)
500g (1lb) blackberries
icing sugar for dusting

1 Preheat the oven to 190C (375F/Gas 5). Butter a 20cm (8 inch) loose-bottomed shallow flan tin. Peel, core and slice the apples and toss in a little lemon juice. Melt 30g (1oz) of the butter in a large sauté pan until sizzling. Add the apples and sprinkle with the sugar. Cook over moderate heat until the apples are just beginning to soften, then turn on to a plate to cool.

2 Melt the remaining butter in a small pan. Brush 1 sheet of filo pastry with melted butter, fold in half and brush again with butter. Lay the filo sheet in the prepared dish so that a corner is at the centre of the dish and the filo overlaps the rim generously on that side. Butter and fold each filo sheet before laying in the tin, overlapping the previous sheet as well as the side of the tin. When you have finished the base should be completely covered and there will be a good overlap all round the tin.

3 Spoon alternate layers of cooked apples and blackberries into the lined tin. Fold the last piece of overlapping filo back over the filling. Repeat with each layer in turn, allowing the filo to form ripples and folds. Brush with a little more butter and dust lightly with icing sugar.

4 Bake in the preheated oven for 45 minutes or until the pastry is crisp and golden brown. Serve dusted with icing sugar. *Serves 8.*

Banana Cream Flan

SWEET PASTRY:
250g (8oz/2 cups) plain flour
pinch of salt
125g (4oz) butter, in pieces
90g (3oz/¹/₃ cup) caster sugar
2 egg yolks
4 teaspoons water
2 drops of vanilla essence
VANILLA CUSTARD:
250ml (8fl oz/1 cup) milk
1 vanilla pod, split
3 egg yolks

45g (1¹/₂oz/3 tbsp) caster sugar
40g (1¹/₄oz/5 tbsp) plain flour
TOPPING:
155ml (5fl oz/²/₃ cup) whipping
cream
1 tablespoon instant coffee
powder
60g (2oz/¹/₄ cup) caster sugar
1 teaspoon rum
3 bananas
juice of ¹/₂ lemon
cocoa powder for dusting

1 Preheat the oven to 180C (350F/Gas 4). Sift the flour and salt into a large bowl. Rub in the butter using the fingertips until the mixture resembles fine breadcrumbs. Stir in the sugar. Mix together the egg yolks, water and vanilla essence and pour over the flour. Mix using a round-bladed knife until the dough clings together. Turn on to a lightly floured surface and knead gently until smooth. Wrap in plastic wrap and chill for 30 minutes.

2 Roll the pastry to a 5mm (¹/₄ inch) thickness and use to line a 20cm (8 inch) flan tin. Prick the base with a fork. Line with a disc of greaseproof paper and dried beans and bake blind for 15 minutes, then remove the beans and cook for 5 minutes until the pastry is dry. Allow to cool.

3 To make the vanilla custard, bring the milk to the boil in a small pan with the vanilla pod added. Whisk the egg yolks and sugar together, then stir in the flour. Stir in a little of the boiling milk, then add to the pan and cook, stirring, for 2-3 minutes until thickened. Allow to cool, then discard the vanilla. Pour into the pastry case and leave until cold.

4 For the topping, whip the cream, adding the coffee, sugar and rum. Slice the bananas, sprinkle with lemon juice and arrange over the custard. Spoon the coffee cream on top. Serve chilled, sprinkled with cocoa. *Serves 6.*

Summer Puddings

1 medium cooking apple
grated rind and juice of
* 1 lemon*
750g (1¹/₂lb) mixed soft fruits,
* eg raspberries, redcurrants,*
* blackcurrants, blackberries,*
* strawberries*

185g (6oz/³/₄ cup) caster sugar
16 thin slices white bread,
* crusts removed*
TO DECORATE:
soft fruits and leaves

1 Peel, core and slice the apple and place in a pan with the lemon rind and juice. Cook gently for about 2-3 minutes until the apple slices are just tender but holding their shape.

2 Prepare the soft fruits, removing the stems and stalks; slice the strawberries. Add the soft fruits to the pan with the sugar and cook gently for about 10 minutes, until the sugar has dissolved and the fruit juices are beginning to run. Remove from the heat.

3 Have ready 6 ramekins or other individual moulds. Measure their inside diameter and, using the same-sized pastry cutter, cut out 12 discs of bread. Press one on to the base of each mould. Cut the remaining bread into strips and use to line the sides.

4 Spoon a little juice from the fruit over the bread in the moulds to give a good red colour. Using a slotted spoon, fill them with the softened fruit and spoon over a little more juice. Top each with another bread round and a spoonful of juice. Strain and reserve the remaining juice.

5 Stand the moulds in a tray, cover with plastic wrap and weigh down each pudding to compress it slightly. Refrigerate overnight.

6 To turn out the puddings, run a small knife around the inside of each dish and invert on to a serving plate. Spoon over the reserved juice and decorate with fruit and leaves. Serve with pouring cream. *Serves 6.*

Apple & Apricot Pancake Layer

As you cook the pancakes, stack them with a sprinkling of sugar between each one to prevent them sticking together.

PANCAKES:
125g (4oz/1 cup) plain flour
pinch of salt
2 teaspoons caster sugar
1 egg
1 egg yolk
315ml (10fl oz/1¼ cups) milk
30g (1 oz) butter, melted
oil for frying

FILLING:
1kg (2lb) apples
250g (8oz/1¾ cups) pre-soaked
  dried apricots, sliced
1 teaspoon ground cinnamon
60g (2oz/⅓ cup) brown sugar
15g (½oz) butter
TO GLAZE:
2 tablespoons apricot jam

1 Preheat the oven to 180C (350F/Gas 4). Grease a 20cm (8 inch) cake tin and line with greaseproof paper. Sift the flour and salt into a large bowl. Add the sugar. Make a well in the centre and add the egg, extra yolk and half the milk. Whisk the liquids together, gradually working in the flour to yield a smooth batter. Add the remaining milk and whisk well. Set aside for 20 minutes.

2 Meanwhile, make the filling. Peel, core and slice the apples and place in a pan with the apricots, cinnamon, sugar and butter. Cook over a low heat, without stirring, for 10-12 minutes until the apples are tender.

3 Add the melted butter to the pancake batter. Lightly oil a small crêpe pan, add a spoonful of batter and swirl the pan to spread the batter. Cook, turning once, to make a thin pancake, no more than 20cm (8 inches) in diameter. Repeat with the remaining batter.

4 Lay one of the pancakes good-side down, in the base of the cake tin. Cover with a thin layer of filling and top with another pancake. Continue layering until all the filling and pancakes are used, finishing with a pancake. Cover with buttered foil and bake in the oven for 10 minutes.

5 Warm the jam with 1 tablespoon water. Turn the dessert on to a warmed serving dish and pour over the glaze. *Serves 6.*

Sticky Toffee Pudding

This delicious pudding tastes equally good hot or cold. I usually serve it hot as a dessert and save any leftovers for tea the next day.

250g (8oz/1½ cups) dates,
   stoned and chopped
1 teaspoon bicarbonate of soda
315ml (10fl oz/1¼ cups)
   boiling water
185g (6oz) butter
185g (6oz/1 cup) soft brown
   sugar
1 egg, lightly beaten

250g (8oz/2 cups) self-raising
   flour
2 drops of vanilla essence
WALNUT TOPPING:
30g (1oz) butter
5 tablespoons soft brown sugar
5 tablespoons double (thick)
   cream
60g (2oz/½ cup) walnuts,
   roughly chopped

1 Preheat the oven to 180C (350F/Gas 4). Grease a 1kg (2lb) loaf tin and line with greaseproof paper, leaving at least 2.5cm (1 inch) overlapping all around (to make it easier to remove the pudding after cooking). Place the dates and bicarbonate of soda in a bowl, pour on the boiling water and allow to stand for 20 minutes.

2 In a bowl, cream the butter and sugar together until fluffy. Add the egg, a little at a time, beating well between each addition. Fold in the flour, vanilla essence and the dates together with their liquid; the batter should be quite runny.

3 Pour the mixture into the prepared tin and bake in the oven for 1 hour until cooked but still moist. If the top appears to be browning too quickly during cooking, cover with foil.

4 For the topping, place the butter, brown sugar and cream in a small pan, bring to the boil and simmer gently for 1 minute. Add the walnuts and keep warm.

5 Carefully lift the cooked pudding out of the tin and place on a warmed serving plate. Remove the paper. Pour the walnut topping over to serve. *Serves 8-10.*

Marmalade & Ginger Pudding

155g (5 oz) butter
155g (5oz/²/₃ cup) caster sugar
2 eggs, lightly beaten
155g (5oz/1¹/₄ cups) self-raising
  flour
2 teaspoons ground ginger

2 tablespoons milk
  (approximately)
250g (8oz/³/₄ cup) marmalade
SAUCE:
2 tablespoons marmalade
juice of 1 orange

1 Grease a 1.25 litre (2 pint/5 cup) pudding basin. In a bowl, cream the butter and sugar together until light and fluffy. Add the eggs, a little at a time, beating well between each addition. Sift the flour and ginger together and fold in, adding enough milk to give a firm dropping consistency.

2 Place the marmalade in the pudding basin and spoon the mixture on top. Cover the basin and cook as for Steamed chocolate pudding (page 54), for 1¹/₄-1¹/₂ hours.

3 Warm the sauce ingredients in a pan. Turn the pudding out on to a warmed dish and pour the sauce over. *Serves 6.*

Rhubarb Oat Crumble

1kg (2lb) rhubarb
185g (6oz/³/₄ cup) caster sugar
grated rind and juice of
  1 orange
TOPPING:
60g (2oz/¹/₂ cup) plain flour
2 teaspoons ground mixed spice

30g (1oz/¹/₄ cup) ground
  almonds
90g (3oz/1 cup) rolled oats
125g (4oz/³/₄ cup) moist light
  brown sugar
125g (4oz) butter, in pieces

1 Preheat the oven to 190C (375F/Gas 5). Cut the rhubarb into 2.5cm (1 inch) batons. Place in a pan with the sugar, orange rind and juice, and cook gently for 5 minutes.

2 To make the topping, in a bowl, mix together the flour, spice, almonds, oats and sugar. Rub in the butter.

3 Place the rhubarb in a 1.25 litre (2 pint/5 cup) ovenproof dish, spoon the crumble mixture over and bake for 40 minutes until golden and crisp. Serve with cream. *Serves 6.*

Steamed Chocolate Pudding

Adding the walnuts gives this deliciously moist pudding an interesting texture. Remember to keep the steamer topped up with water during cooking.

125g (4oz) plain (dark)
  chocolate
1 tablespoon milk
125g (4oz) butter
125g (4oz/³/₄ cup) soft brown
  sugar
2 eggs, lightly beaten

90 g (3 oz/³/₄ cup) self-raising
  flour
60g (2oz/1 cup) fresh
  breadcrumbs
30g (1oz/¹/₄ cup) walnuts,
  chopped

1 Lightly butter a 1.25 litre (2 pint/5 cup) pudding basin. Melt the chocolate together with the milk in a small bowl over a pan of hot water.

2 In a bowl, cream the butter and sugar together until light and fluffy. Add the eggs, a little at a time, beating well between each addition. Fold in the melted chocolate, flour, breadcrumbs and chopped walnuts, using a metal spoon.

3 Spoon the mixture into the pudding basin, cover with a double layer of buttered greaseproof paper or foil and tie securely with string. Put the basin in the top of a steamer. Cover and steam for 2 hours, topping up the boiling water as necessary.

4 Remove the paper or foil and turn out the pudding on to a warmed serving plate. Serve with cream or custard. *Serves 6.*

NOTE: If you do not have a steamer, put the basin into a large saucepan containing enough boiling water to come one third of the way up the basin. Cover and boil steadily for 1½ hours, topping up with boiling water as necessary.

Chocolate Truffle Pie

This one is for all the chocoholics I know. Once tasted, never forgotten.

60g (2oz/1/2 cup) plain flour
30g (1oz/1/4 cup) cocoa powder
3 eggs
90g (3oz/1/3 cup) caster sugar
SYRUP:
60g (2oz/1/4 cup) caster sugar
100ml (3 1/2fl oz/1/2 cup) water
1 tablespoon grand marnier

TOPPING:
470g (15oz) plain (dark)
    chocolate, in pieces
470ml (15fl oz/1 3/4 cups)
    whipping cream
cocoa powder for dusting

1 Preheat the oven to 180C (350F/Gas 4). Grease the base and side of a 25cm (10 inch) spring form cake tin and line the base with greaseproof paper. Dust the tin with a little flour. Sift together the flour and cocoa.

2 Place the eggs and sugar in a large bowl over a pan of hot water. Whisk continuously with an electric whisk or a large balloon whisk until the mixture is very thick and has trebled in volume. Remove from the heat and whisk until cool. Lightly fold in the flour and cocoa; do not over-mix. Pour the mixture into the prepared tin and bake for 20 minutes until a skewer inserted in the centre comes out clean. Turn out and cool on a wire rack.

3 To make the syrup, put the ingredients in a small pan, bring slowly to the boil and simmer for 1 minute. Cool.

4 Slice the cake in half horizontally. Place one layer, cut side up, in the cake tin and moisten with the syrup. (Freeze the other cake layer for later use).

5 To make the topping, melt the chocolate in a bowl over a pan of hot water. Whisk the cream until it begins to leave a ribbon, pour in the melted chocolate and whisk to mix; do not over-whisk. Pour into the cake tin, smooth the top and chill for 2 hours.

6 To serve, dip a small knife into boiling water and run it around the inside of the cake tin, then remove the tin. Dust the top with cocoa. *Serves 8-10*.

White Chocolate Mousse

A smooth white chocolate mousse served in dark chocolate cups for added contrast. If you are short of time, ready-made chocolate cups can be bought from most supermarkets.

185g (6oz) plain (dark)
   chocolate, in pieces
WHITE CHOCOLATE MOUSSE:
185g (6oz) white chocolate,
   in pieces
185g (6oz) butter, in pieces

3 egg yolks
2 egg whites
125g (4 oz/½ cup) caster sugar
TO DECORATE:
chocolate shapes or grated
   chocolate

1 Put the chocolate into a small bowl over a pan of hot water; when melted, remove the bowl from the heat and stir until smooth.

2 Have ready 16 paper cake cases. Using either the end of a spoon or your forefinger, carefully spread a thin layer of the chocolate in each paper case to line completely. Set aside in a cool place to harden.

3 Put the white chocolate and butter together in a bowl over a pan of hot water. When melted, remove from the heat and beat with an electric whisk. Add the egg yolks one at a time beating constantly; do not be surprised if the mixture separates at this stage. Continue beating until the mixture becomes creamy and very thick.

4 Whisk the egg whites in a bowl until stiff peaks form. Add the sugar a little at a time, whisking constantly, until stiff glossy peaks form. Stir a spoonful of this meringue into the chocolate mixture to lighten it, then fold in the remainder.

5 Carefully spoon the mixture into the prepared chocolate cases and chill for several hours until set.

6 To serve, decorate with grated chocolate or shapes. *Serves 8.*

NOTE: Using melted chocolate in a greaseproof paper piping bag, you can pipe simple outlines on to non-stick paper. Allow to set before removing.

Roulade with Cherries

This moist chocolate sponge wrapped around cherries and kirsch is an adaptation of the traditional Black Forest gâteau.

185g (6oz) plain (dark)
  chocolate, in pieces
2 tablespoons brandy
5 eggs, separated
185 (6oz/³⁄₄ cup) caster sugar

FILLING:
315ml (10fl oz/1¹⁄₄ cups) double
  (thick) cream
440g (14oz) can black cherries
2 tablespoons kirsch
TO SERVE:
icing sugar for dusting

1 Preheat the oven to 180C (350F/Gas 4). Line a 33 × 23 cm (13 × 9 inch) Swiss roll tin with greaseproof paper and brush lightly with oil.

2 Melt the chocolate in a bowl over a pan of simmering water. Remove from the heat and stir in the brandy.

3 In a bowl, beat the egg yolks and sugar together until thick and light. Fold in the chocolate mixture. In a separate bowl, whisk the egg whites until they form stiff peaks. Stir a spoonful into the chocolate mixture to lighten it, then fold in the remainder.

4 Pour the mixture into the prepared tin and bake for 20 minutes. Cover with a clean tea towel and allow to cool in the tin.

5 Whip the cream until it forms soft peaks. Drain, halve and stone the cherries, reserving the syrup. Fold them into the cream with the kirsch and a little of the cherry syrup.

6 Dust a large piece of greaseproof paper generously with icing sugar. Turn the roulade out on to the paper with a long side facing you. Peel off the lining paper and trim the sides. Spread the roulade evenly with the cream to within 2.5cm (1 inch) of the long side farthest from you. Using the paper to help you, roll the roulade away from you as tightly and evenly as possible.

7 Chill for at least 2 hours before serving, sprinkled liberally with icing sugar. *Serves 8.*

Crunchy Chocolate Fudge Cake

A version of an American refrigerator cake. This one is simple to make and keeps well, although in my house it never stays around very long!

60g (2oz) butter
500g (1lb) plain (dark)
  chocolate
75ml (2½fl oz/⅓ cup) strong
  black coffee
1 tablespoon golden syrup
1 tablespoon rum
125g (4oz/¾ cup) mixed nuts
  (almonds, hazelnuts, walnuts)

250g (8oz) shortbread
125g (4oz/¾ cup) dates, stoned
  and chopped
125g (4oz/¾ cup) glacé cherries,
  halved
1 banana, roughly chopped
TO DECORAATE:
6 glacé cherries
angelica diamonds

1 Grease a 750g (1½lb) loaf tin. Place the butter, chocolate, coffee, golden syrup and rum in a heatproof bowl over a pan of simmering water and heat gently until the chocolate is melted. Remove from the heat and stir until smooth.
2 Roughly break up the nuts and half of the shortbread. Crush the remaining shortbread.
3 Add the dates, cherries, banana, nuts and all of the shortbread to the chocolate mixture and stir until evenly mixed. Spoon into the prepared tin. Press down well into the corners, level the top, cover and refrigerate overnight.
4 To serve, run the point of a small knife around the sides of the tin and invert on to a serving plate. Decorate the top with halved cherries and angelica leaves. Cut into thin slices, using a sharp knife, to serve. *Serves 8.*

Iced Chocolate Terrine

When melting chocolate over a bain marie, or a pan of hot water, it is important that the temperature of the chocolate does not exceed 35C (85F) otherwise it will spoil.

60g (2oz/¹⁄₃ cup) prunes, pitted
60g (2oz/¹⁄₃ cup) dates, pitted
60ml (2fl oz/¹⁄₄ cup) brandy
100ml (3¹⁄₂fl oz/¹⁄₄ cup) hot
*   black tea*
315ml (10fl oz/1¹⁄₄ cups) double
*   (thick) cream*

375g (12oz) plain (dark)
*   chocolate*
90g (3oz) butter
3 egg yolks
2 egg whites
2 teaspoons caster sugar
TO DECORATE:
2-3 plums, stoned and sliced

1 Put the prunes and dates in a bowl. Pour the brandy and tea over them, stir and leave to soak overnight.

2 Drain the fruits and chop roughly; reserve the liquor.

3 Whip half of the cream until soft peaks form and spread evenly over the base and sides of a 940ml (1½ pint/3¾ cup) terrine. Place in the freezer until firm.

4 Melt the chocolate and butter in a heatproof bowl over a pan of hot water. Stir in the egg yolks, soaked fruit and about half of the reserved liquor; the mixture should be fairly stiff.

5 Whip the remaining cream until it forms soft peaks. In another bowl, whisk the egg whites until stiff, then add the sugar, whisking constantly until glossy peaks form. Stir a spoonful of the cream into the chocolate mixture to lighten it. Fold in the remaining cream, then fold in the egg whites.

6 Pour this mixture into the cream-lined terrine, cover with plastic wrap and freeze for 3-4 hours or until firm.

7 To serve, run the point of a knife around the inside of the terrine and dip it briefly in hot water. Invert on to a chilled plate and slice thinly with a sharp knife. Serve decorated with plum slices. *Serves 8-10.*

Yogurt & Honey Ice with Tuiles

The inspiration for this dish came from sitting in Greek tavernas on sun-baked afternoons eating yogurt drizzled with honey. Experiment with flavoured honeys, such as acacia, lavender or clover.

315ml (10fl oz/1¼ cups) milk
4 egg yolks
155ml (5fl oz/²/₃ cup) honey
185ml (6fl oz/³/₄ cup) Greek
*   yogurt*
315ml (10fl oz/1¼ cups)
*   whipping cream, lightly*
*   whipped*
extra honey to serve

TUILES:
125g (4oz/1 cup) chopped
*   almonds*
30g (1oz/¼ cup) plain flour
125g (4oz/³/₄ cup) icing sugar
2 drops of orange flower water
2 egg whites
60g (2oz) butter, melted and
*   cooled*

1 To make the ice cream, bring the milk to the boil in a saucepan. In a bowl, whisk together the egg yolks and honey until thick and light. Stir a little of the hot milk into the whisked mixture, then add to the milk in the pan and cook over a low heat, stirring constantly, until thick enough to coat the back of the spoon; do not boil. Cool.

2 Fold the yogurt and cream into the cooled custard. Pour into an ice cream machine and churn until thick, then transfer to a freezerproof container and freeze until required. Alternatively, pour into a shallow tray and freeze, beating twice during freezing.

3 To make the tuiles, preheat the oven to 200C (400F/Gas 6) and lightly grease 2 baking sheets. Mix the almonds, flour and icing sugar in a bowl. Add the remaining ingredients and stir until smooth; chill for 10 minutes.

4 Spoon the mixture into mounds on the baking sheets, spacing well apart. Spread into thin rounds. Bake for 5 minutes until pale golden. Allow to cool slightly before carefully lifting over a rolling pin. Remove when cold.

5 To serve, scoop the ice cream on to serving plates, drizzle a little honey over the top and serve with the tuiles. *Serves 6.*

Rhubarb Sorbet

Sorbets look most attractive scooped into glass dishes and served decorated with a little of the poached fruit.

500g (1lb) rhubarb, trimmed
grated rind and juice of
    1 orange
90ml (3fl oz/¹/₃ cup) water
125g (4oz/¹/₂ cup) caster sugar

2 teaspoons powdered gelatine,
    soaked in 2 tablespoons water
2 drops of red food colouring
    (optional)
1 egg white, lightly whisked

1 Cut rhubarb into small pieces. Place in a pan with the orange rind and juice, water and sugar. Cover and cook gently for 5-10 minutes or until tender. Add the gelatine; it will dissolve immediately. Purée in a blender or food processor. Add colouring, if required.

2 Transfer to an ice cream machine and churn until slushy. Add the egg white and continue to churn until thick and almost set. Freeze in a freezerproof container until required. Alternatively, freeze in a shallow tray until slushy, add the beaten egg white and whisk until smooth. Freeze until firm, beating once more during freezing. *Serves 4-6.*

Gooseberry & Elder Sorbet

750g (1¹/₂lb) gooseberries,
    topped and tailed
4 heads elderflower
625ml (20fl oz/2¹/₂ cups) water

315g (10oz/1¹/₄ cups) caster
    sugar
grated rind and juice of
    2 lemons

1 Place the gooseberries, elderflower heads and 2 table-spoons water in a large pan. Cover and simmer gently until the fruit is soft. Discard the elderflowers, then pass the fruit through a nylon sieve. Set aside to cool.

2 Put the sugar and remaining water in a large pan and heat slowly to dissolve the sugar. Bring to the boil and cook for 1 minute. Allow to cool, then add to the fruit purée with the lemon rind and juice. Freeze and serve as above. *Serves 8.*

Frozen Strawberry Yogurt

This recipe can be adapted to suit most soft fruits; try using apricots, mango or even banana. Although ice creams will keep for several weeks in the freezer, they always taste better a day or two after you make them.

125g (4oz/½ cup) caster sugar
250ml (8fl oz/1 cup) water
500g (1lb) strawberries
315ml (10fl oz/1¼ cups) thick
  strawberry yogurt

155ml (5fl oz/⅔ cup) double
  (thick) cream
1 egg white

1 Put the sugar and water in a saucepan and heat gently until the sugar has dissolved. Bring to the boil and boil steadily until the syrup registers 107C (225F) on a sugar thermometer, or until a little of the syrup forms a thread when pressed between a wet thumb and forefinger and drawn apart.

2 Set aside a few strawberries for decoration; roughly chop a further 60g (2oz). Place the remainder in a blender or food processor with the sugar syrup and work to a purée. Transfer to a bowl and allow to cool. Fold in the yogurt.

3 Transfer the mixture to an ice cream machine and churn until beginning to set. Whip the cream until soft peaks form. In another bowl, whisk the egg white to the same stage. Fold both into the frozen mixture with the chopped strawberries. Continue to churn until firm, then transfer to a freezerproof container and freeze until firm.

4 Alternatively, pour the yogurt and strawberry mixture into a shallow tray and freeze until beginning to set. Transfer to a chilled bowl and beat until smooth. Fold in the whipped cream and whisked egg white and return to the freezer until firm.

5 To serve, scoop into glass serving dishes and decorate with the reserved strawberries. *Serves 6.*

Cinnamon Ice & Calvados Apples

Apples and cinnamon have always been a great partnership. Here an unusual cinnamon ice cream is complemented by hot calvados-flavoured apples.

500ml (16fl oz/2 cups) milk
6 cinnamon sticks
6 egg yolks
125g (4oz/½ cup) caster sugar
1 teaspoon ground cinnamon
250ml (8fl oz/1 cup) whipping cream, lightly whipped
TO SERVE:
ground cinnamon for sprinkling

CALVADOS APPLES:
2 Bramley's or other cooking apples
30g (1oz) butter
1-2 teaspoons lemon juice
30g (1oz/5 teaspoons) caster sugar
dash of calvados

1 Place the milk and cinnamon sticks in a small pan and bring to the boil. Beat the egg yolks with the sugar until light, then stir in a little of the hot milk. Add to the milk in the saucepan and cook, stirring constantly, until thickened; do not boil. Allow to cool.

2 Remove the cinnamon sticks from the custard and stir in the ground cinnamon.

3 Transfer to an ice cream machine and churn for 20 minutes, until quite thick. Add the cream and churn for a further 10 minutes or until set. Alternatively, pour the custard into a shallow freezerproof tray and freeze until ice crystals begin to form around the edge; remove from the freezer and beat for 1 minute. Continue freezing, beating twice more until half-set. Turn into a bowl and beat in the cream. Transfer the ice cream to a freezerproof container and freeze until firm.

4 Peel, core and thickly slice the apples. Heat the butter in a frying pan until sizzling. Add the apples, sprinkle with lemon juice and sugar and sauté over a high heat for 2-3 minutes until soft. Add a little calvados and flambé.

5 Scoop the ice cream on to serving plates and surround with the hot apples. Sprinkle with cinnamon. *Serves 4.*

Lemon Curd Ice in Baskets

LEMON CURD ICE:
6 egg yolks
2 egg whites
125g (4oz) butter
315g (10oz/1¼ cups) caster
  sugar
grated rind and juice of
  3 lemons
625ml (20fl oz/2½ cups) double
  (thick) cream
625ml (20fl oz/2½ cups) Greek
  yogurt

CANDIED LEMON ZEST:
shredded rind of 1 lemon
1 tablespoon caster sugar
2 tablespoons water
BRANDY SNAPS BASKETS:
60g (2oz/½ cup) plain flour
1 teaspoon ground ginger
60g (2oz) butter
125g (4oz/½ cup) caster sugar
2 tablespoons golden syrup
TO DECORATE:
mint sprigs

1 Lightly mix together the egg yolks and whites, strain. Melt the butter in a bowl over a pan of boiling water, add the sugar, eggs and rind and juice of 2 lemons. Stir constantly until the mixture thickens. Allow to cool.

2 Whip the cream until it is the same consistency as the yogurt. Stir a little of each into the lemon curd to lighten it. Fold in the remainder, together with the juice and rind of the remaining lemon. Freeze until required.

3 For the candied lemon zest, put the ingredients in a pan and cook until beginning to caramelize. Cool.

4 Preheat the oven to 200C (400F/Gas 6). Grease 2 large baking sheets and oil 2 oranges (for moulding the brandy snap baskets). Sift together the flour and ginger. Cream the butter until soft and light, then add the sugar, golden syrup and flour. Mix to a smooth dough. Chill for 20 minutes.

5 Form the dough into 8 balls. Place one in the centre of each baking sheet and cook for 8-10 minutes until golden and bubbling. Allow to cool for 1 minute, then carefully remove with a palette knife and place each one over an orange, gently pressing the sides to form folds. Allow to cool before removing. Repeat to make 8 baskets.

6 To serve, fill each basket with lemon ice and top with candied lemon zest and mint. *Serves 8.*

Iced Cointreau Soufflé

This refreshing dessert can be prepared in advance and left in the
freezer for several days until required.

3 eggs
2 egg yolks
155g (5oz/²/₃ cup) caster sugar
grated rind and juice of
    1 orange

315ml (10fl oz/1¼ cups)
    whipping cream
75ml (2½fl oz/⅓ cup) cointreau
cocoa powder for dusting

1 First prepare a 625ml (1 pint/2½ cup) soufflé dish. Cut a
piece of non-stick paper long enough to wrap around the dish
and at least 25cm (10 inches) deep. Fold in half lengthways to
give a 12cm (5 inch) band. Carefully wrap this around the
soufflé dish and secure with a piece of string. The collar
should stand about 5cm (2 inches) above the top of the dish.
2 Place the whole eggs, extra yolks, sugar, orange rind and
juice in a large heatproof bowl. Stand the bowl over a pan of
hot water and whisk continuously using an electric whisk if
possible, until the mixture forms a thick ribbon when the
whisk is lifted.
3 Remove the bowl from the pan and whisk until the mixture
is cool.
4 Whip the cream until it is the same consistency as the
whisked mixture, then fold a spoonful of cream into the mixture to lighten it. Fold in the remaining cream, together with
the cointreau. Pour the mixture into the prepared soufflé dish
and place in the freezer overnight.
5 To serve, carefully remove the paper collar, smooth the
edge and dust the top with a layer of cocoa. *Serves 10.*

Bombe Tutti Frutti

TUTTI FRUTTI ICE CREAM:
30g (1oz/¹/₄ cup) dried apricots
30g (1oz/¹/₄ cup) maraschino
  cherries, drained and chopped
30g (1oz/¹/₄ cup) raisins
30g (1oz/¹/₄ cup) candied fruits,
  chopped
2 tablespoons brandy
2 eggs, separated
45g (1¹/₂oz/6¹/₂ tsp) caster sugar
30g (1oz/¹/₄ cup) flaked almonds

155ml (5fl oz/²/₃ cup) double
  (thick) cream, softly whipped
VANILLA ICE CREAM:
250ml (8fl oz/1 cup) milk
1 vanilla pod, split
3 egg yolks
60g (2oz/¹/₄ cup) caster sugar
250ml (8fl oz/1 cup) double
  (thick) cream, softly whipped
TO DECORATE:
crystallized fruits and angelica

1 Chill a 940ml (1½ pint/3¾ cup) bombe mould. Soak the apricots in boiling water to cover until well swollen; drain and chop. Place in a bowl with the cherries, raisins, candied fruits and brandy. Leave for several hours or overnight. Drain, reserving 1 teaspoon juice.

2 Whisk the egg whites until stiff, then gradually whisk in the sugar to yield a stiff, glossy meringue. Fold into the whipped cream with the egg yolks, almonds, soaked fruits and reserved juice. Spread the mixture around the base and sides of the bombe mould. Freeze until firm.

3 To make the vanilla ice cream, put the milk in a small pan with the vanilla pod and bring to the boil. Whisk together the egg yolks and sugar until thick and light. Stir in a little of the hot milk, then add to the milk in the pan and cook, stirring, until thick enough to coat the back of the spoon; do not boil. Allow to cool, then discard the vanilla pod.

4 Freeze the custard in a shallow tray until crystals form round the edges, then remove from the freezer and beat until smooth. Freeze until almost set, beat once more, then fold in the whipped cream and freeze until just firm.

5 Fill the centre of the bombe with the vanilla ice cream, cover and freeze overnight.

6 To serve, dip bombe into hot water and invert on to a plate. Decorate with crystallized fruits and angelica. *Serves 8.*

Index